Scrub-a-Du

Written by Elspeth Graham
Illustrated by Mal Peet

Collins Educational
An Imprint of HarperCollinsPublishers

600 years ago

Medieval towns were dirty, smelly places. People threw their rubbish and emptied their lavatory buckets into the street.

Most people living in Medieval times were smelly, too. They very rarely had a bath as it was such hard work. Women had to carry buckets and buckets of water from the well. Then they had to spend hours heating the water in pots over the fire.

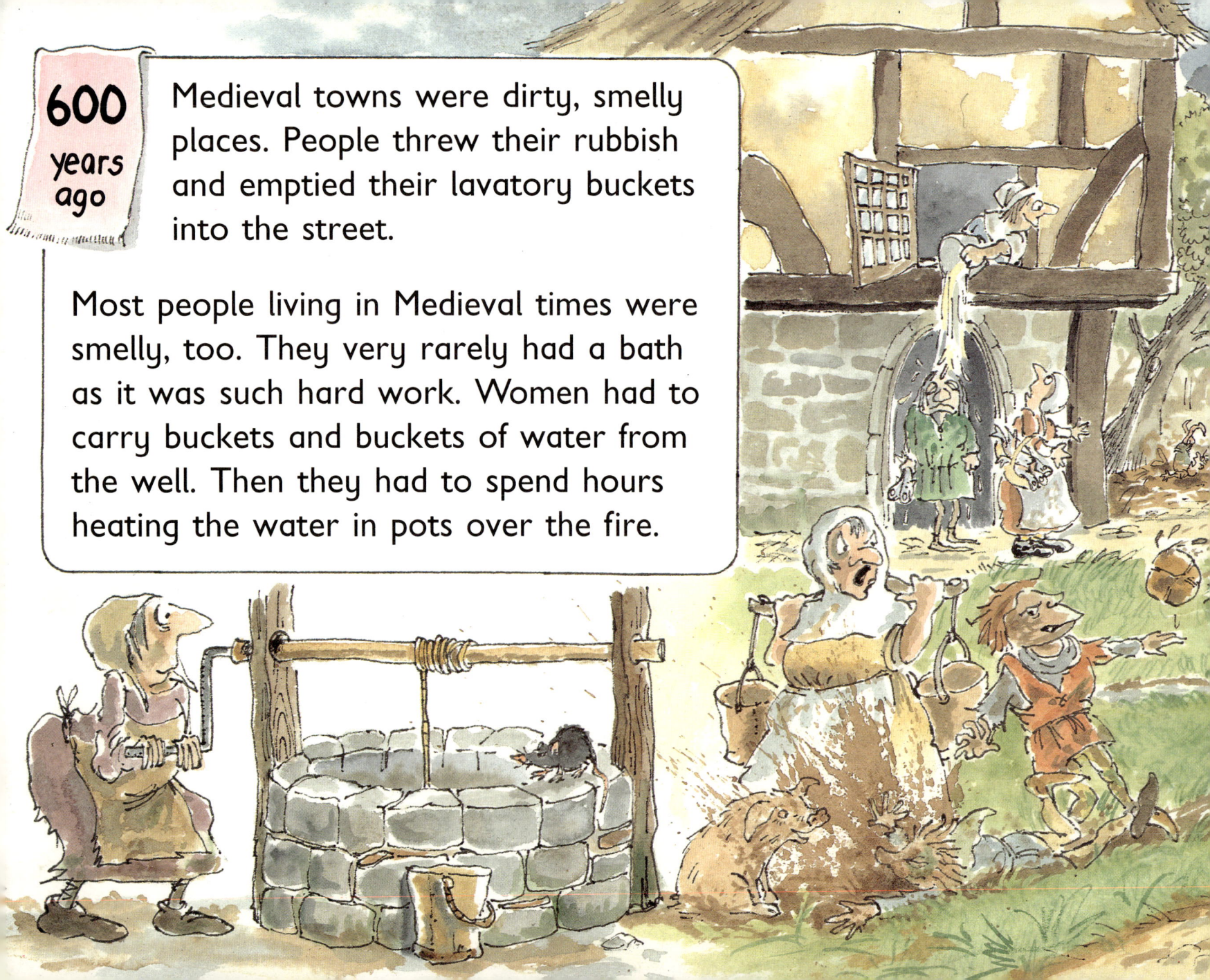

Rich lords and ladies were usually a bit cleaner than other people. Their castles were cold and draughty but they did have a bath now and again. Of course, these rich people had servants to fetch and heat the water.

400 years ago

Doctors had different ideas about baths. Some of them believed that having a bath was so dangerous that a doctor had to be present. Others believed that bathing could cure just about anything. Some doctors said that you must always bathe in cold water. Others said you should bathe only in hot water.

An Italian doctor called Sanctorius was so sure that bathing was good for sick people that he invented the **bag bath.** His patients could have a bath without getting out of bed.

220 years ago

An Englishman called Doctor John Graham had a bath-house in London where very peculiar things went on. Doctor Graham believed that bathing in soil was good for you. He and his patients used to sit buried up to the neck in soil for four hours at a time. People paid to come in and watch. One day a farmer poured water over Doctor Graham's head to see if he would grow.

 **100 years ago**

In Victorian times people discovered that dirt could spread disease and illness, and they began to realize how important it was to keep clean. So the Victorians began to build proper bathrooms in their houses. Some of these bathrooms were very fancy indeed.

Only a few very rich people had a fantastic bathroom like this. Thousands of poor families lived in houses without proper toilets or bathrooms or even running water. They would have been amazed at a bathroom like this one.

Wow!

100 years ago The Victorians invented all sorts of bathing machines.

This is a **pedal shower.**

With this machine, you could exercise and have a cold shower at the same time. The pedals worked a pump which pushed water up to the top of the shower. The harder you pedalled, the faster the shower worked.

This is a **gas-fired bath.**

It had a gas burner under one end...

BOOM!

...which sounds rather dangerous.

15